C000221630

Text: *Vivienne Crow*

Photographs: *Vivienne Crow, Carl Rogers, Shutterstock, Stewart Smith Photography*

Design: *Carl Rogers*

© Northern Eye Books Limited 2022

Northern Eye Books
ISBN 978-1-914589-14-0

A CIP catalogue record for this book is available from the British Library

www.northerneyebooks.co.uk

Cover: *Sunrise over Blea Tarn (Walk 4)*

Important Advice: The routes described in this book are undertaken at the reader's own risk. Walkers should take into account their level of fitness, wear suitable footwear and clothing, and carry food and water. It is also advisable to take the relevant OS map with you in case you get lost and leave the area covered by our maps.

Whilst every care has been taken to ensure the accuracy of the route directions, the publishers cannot accept responsibility for errors or omissions, or for changes in the details given. Nor can the publisher and copyright owners accept responsibility for any consequences arising from the use of this book.

If you find any inaccuracies in either the text or maps, please write or email us at the address below. Thank you.

First edition published 2015
This 2nd fully revised edition published 2022

Northern Eye Books Limited
Northern Eye Books, Tattenhall, Cheshire CH3 9PX
Email: tony@northerneyebooks.co.uk
For sales enquiries, please call 01928 723 744

  @northerneyebooks

 @viviennecrow2
@Northerneyeboo

MIX
Paper from responsible sources
FSC® C016379
www.fsc.org

Printed and bound in the UK by Charlesworth Press

Contents

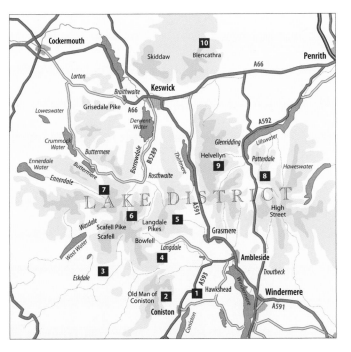

England's Largest National Park

THE LAKE DISTRICT NATIONAL PARK is the largest and most popular of the thirteen National Parks in England and Wales. Created as one of Britain's first National Parks in 1951, its role is to 'conserve and enhance' the natural beauty, wildlife and culture of this iconic English landscape, not just for residents and visitors today but for future generations, too.

Remarkably, the National Park contains every scrap of England's land over 3,000 feet, including its highest mountain, Scafell Pike. Packed within the Park's 912 square miles are numerous peaks and fells, over 400 lakes and tarns, around 50 dales, six National Nature Reserves, and more than 100 Sites of Special Scientific Interest—all publicly accessible on nearly 2,000 miles of footpaths and other rights of way. It's no surprise then, that the Lake District attracts an estimated 15 million visitors a year.

Early morning at Tarn Hows

Lake District Tarns

Norsemen, who dominated Lakeland 1,000 years ago, called the small bodies of water they found in the mountains *tjorns*—'little lakes' or , literally, 'teardrops'. Now known as tarns, they are remnants of the last Ice Age when huge ice sheets scoured out hollows in the mountains that then filled with water.

There are hundreds of tarns in the National Park: from tiny pools sparkling like blue jewels on high, lonely ridge tops, to small lakes sitting cold and moody at the base of sombre cliffs.

"Beneath our feet, a little lowly vale...
A liquid pool that glittered in the sun,
... Ah! what a sweet Recess, thought I, is here."

William Wordsworth, *The Excursion*, 1814

TOP 10 **Walks:** Walks to Tarns

THERE ARE LITERALLY HUNDREDS of tarns scattered throughout the Lake District, each with its own special character. The ten in this book have been chosen for their moody locations, their dramatic backdrops, and the superb walks to get to them. Some are enclosed within high mountain combes, while others are cradled on low-lying hills; some are en-route to popular summits, others are off the beaten track. Yet each of them will provide walkers with memories to cherish for a lifetime.

Tarn Hows page 8

Levers Water page 14

Eel & Burnmoor Tarns page 18

Blea Tarn page 24

Tall pines frame the view at Tarn Hows

Tarn Hows

A gentle saunter through undulating woods to one of Lakeland's most popular beauty spots

What to expect:
Field and woodland paths, some tracks

Distance/time: 9.5 kilometres/ 6 miles. Allow 2½-3 hours

Start: Pay and Display car park beside the Tourist Information Centre in the centre of Coniston

Grid ref: SD 303 975

Ordnance Survey Map: OL 7 *The English Lakes South-eastern area Windermere, Kendal and Silverdale*

After the walk: Pubs, cafés and tearooms in Coniston

Walk outline

Starting from Coniston, this straightforward walk follows a series of paths across fields and through woods to the beautifully situated Tarn Hows. A constructed track does a circuit of this delightful body of water, after which the route descends beside the pretty cascades of Tom Gill. A series of farm paths, woodland trails and quiet lanes then returns the walker to Coniston.

Tarn Hows

Despite being man-made, Tarn Hows is well worth a visit. There used to be three tiny tarns here, but the single body of water you see today was created when the 19th-century industrialist James Marshall dammed one of them. With plans based on ideas of the 'picturesque' that were popular at the time, he wanted to create something beautiful. In so doing, he also planted the conifers surrounding the tarn, a feature that is intended both to frame and dramatically reveal views of his creation.

Tom Gill

Waterlily

A winter sunset illuminates the slopes of Tom Heights

The Walk

1. Leave the car park, go briefly left along Ruskin Avenue and then right along the **B5285** (**Tilberthwaite Avenue**). Nearing the edge of **Coniston** and immediately before a **bridge**, turn left into **Shepherds Bridge Lane**.

Opposite the primary school, take the signed footpath over the bridge on the right. Immediately after crossing, turn left along the bank to enter fields. The path heads off across the field, passing beneath a line of oaks and towards a **stone-built folly**.

This Gothic construction is probably the grandest kennel you will ever see. It was built by James Marshall, who was also responsible for creating Tarn Hows, after he became master of the Coniston foxhounds in 1839.

The path continues through a gate beside the folly on a gentle rise. After the next gate, bear left at a waymarked fork. Enter the woods by a kissing-gate surrounded by ancient yew trees. Follow the path through the next field and, on the far side, drop left to go through a gate. The path cuts directly through the next field aiming for a kissing-gate in a fence. This leads onto a farm track. Turn left here.

2. Follow the track to an **old stone bridge** but don't cross it; instead, go through the kissing-gate into the field directly ahead (signed to 'Tarn Hows'). Walk along the field edge to enter woods again by a kissing-gate next to **Yewdale Beck**. The path keeps beside the beck briefly, before veering right to climb through the trees. Go through a gate and turn right along the sealed track. On reaching a lane, turn left and follow it towards **Tarn Hows**.

Hidden from view until the last moment, Tarn Hows sits in a hollow surrounded by woods

and low-lying fells. To the west, Wetherlam and the Coniston fells provide a craggy backdrop to the scene.

3. Opposite the pedestrian entrance to the **Tarn Hows car park**, turn left on to a footpath and keep right when it quickly splits. A path then joins from the left. At a fork, keep right, along the higher route. The path drops back to tarn level, crosses a bridge and goes through a gate.

A view across Tarn Hows to Wetherlam and the Coniston fells

4. About 800 metres after passing, and ignoring, a path to Skelwith Bridge on the right — and immediately before the tarnside route crosses the outflow — take the trail on the right. This hugs the rocky side of the beck which steepens into a series of picturesque cascades beyond a kissing-gate. The climax is **Tom Gill waterfall**, a modest affair by Lakeland standards, set amid oak woods. About 500 metres after leaving the tarn, bear left to drop back on to the beckside path and follow this downstream.

5. Nearing the road, turn left over a **footbridge** and through the car park.

On the far side of the second, smaller section of the car park, a permissive path crosses a bridge and enters a field to run parallel to the **A593**. Just beyond **Yew Tree Farm** on the opposite side, go through the kissing-gate on the right, turn right along the road and then head left along the farm's access lane.

6. Take the **signed bridleway** to the right of the farm. At a fork, bear left, coming away from the wall.

7. At a narrow lane turn left over the **little stone bridge** and then bear right along the bridleway, continuing parallel to the road. At the **Tilberthwaite lane**,

go left and immediately right to walk through woods below **Yewdale Fells**.

8. Leave the trees by a gate in the wall ahead and, in 150 metres, go left through a second gate. Walk down to the lane and turn right. At the next junction, cross diagonally left into **Shepherds Bridge Lane**. Retrace the outward route to complete the walk. ♦

Monk Coniston estate

Tarn Hows is part of the Monk Coniston estate bought by James Marshall in 1835. In 1926, the hall and gardens were sold to John Bradshaw. Beatrix Potter bought the rest of the estate, including Tarn Hows, in 1930. She then sold half at cost price to the National Trust; the other half passed to the charity after her death in 1943. The National Trust reunited the estate in 1945 by purchasing the hall and gardens.

Cloud over Levers Water

Levers Water

A moderate walk up to a glacial basin at the craggy base of the Coniston fells

What to expect:
Beckside path, old mine tracks and gentle descent

Distance/time: 7 kilometres/ 4½miles. Allow 2½-3½ hours

Start: Main Pay and Display car park near the Tourist Information Centre in Coniston

Grid ref: SD 303 975

Ordnance Survey Map: OL 6 *The English Lakes North-western area. Coniston, Ulverston & Barrow-in-Furness*

After the walk: Wide choice of pubs and cafés in Coniston

Walk outline

This walk makes use of miners' tracks in the Coppermines Valley. The route is reasonably straightforward, although the path leading away from Levers Water and into the magnificent Boulder Valley can be a little hard to find, and some of the tracks can be annoyingly stony at times. There are one or two moderately steep climbs, but these are short-lived.

Levers Water

Levers Water sits glittering in a glacial bowl at the foot of the Coniston fells. It started life as a natural tarn, although it was dammed and enlarged to provide water for the mines. Its status today as a reservoir though doesn't detract from the grandeur of its setting.

The walk passes through a landscape dotted with the remains of Coniston's ancient copper mining industry. While industrial archaeology enthusiasts marvel at how the German miners of the 16th- and 17th-centuries managed to work the seams before the days of Victorian engineering, others will be spellbound by the craggy fells on all sides.

Coppermines Valley

Meadow pipit

The Walk

1. Leave the car park, turn left along the residential road and left along the B5285. At the T-junction, turn left again, then take the road on the right. Turn right along the lane after the Sun Hotel. Go through the gate at the top to access a rough track that soon climbs alongside **Church Beck**.

2. Cross the beck via **Miners Bridge** and turn left to continue upstream. Follow the track as it passes in front of the **Coppermines Youth Hostel** (formerly the old mine office) and then climbs beside a waterfall. When the track forks about 400 metres beyond the hostel, bear right. (You will see the water treatment works just down to

your left here.) Almost immediately, turn right up a grassy path, which provides a brief but welcome respite from the stony track. This soon swings left as it joins a path coming in from the right. Continue uphill on rejoining the main track.

3. When you finally reach **Levers Water**, turn left to cross the dam. Follow the water's edge for a short while and then bear left at a fork in the path—up towards some fenced workings.

This dangerous area is known as the **Back Strings** and forms part of the original copper workings by the German miners.

4. Immediately after a second fenced area, turn left to head up the slope, at first with the fence on your left. You will soon pick up a clearer path that takes you down into **Boulder Valley** at the foot of **Brim Fell**'s steep eastern slopes.

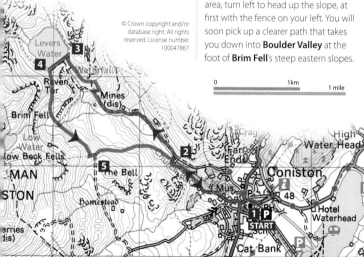

Levers Water started life as a natural tarn but was enlarged by miners

After crossing a bridge over **Low Water Beck**, you pass a huge boulder known as the **Pudding Stone**.

5. Turn left at a T-junction and then, almost immediately, bear left along the lower of the two tracks. You will eventually see **Church Beck** again down to your left. Keep left at a fork in the path near **Miners' Bridge**, but don't cross the bridge. From here it's simply a case of retracing your steps to the car park, remembering to turn left at the Sun Hotel, left at the T-junction and then immediately right at **St Andrew's Church**, to complete the walk. ♦

Coppermines Valley

There is evidence of copper mining in Coniston as far back as 1599, soon after German miners were invited to England by Elizabeth I. Employed by the Company of Mines Royal, they established copper and lead mines throughout Cumbria. Most of the workings passed on this walk date from the 19th century, but the remains of earlier mines, including the Back Strings (left), can be seen near Levers Water.

Eel Tarn with Harter Fell in the background

Eel & Burnmoor Tarns

A visit to two little-visited tarns in one of the Lake District's quietest, but most beautiful valleys

What to expect:
Road; good tracks; open moorland, sometimes boggy

Distance/time: 9.5 kilometres/ 6 miles. Allow 3-3½ hours
Total ascent: 260m/853ft
Start: Dalegarth Station, Eskdale – the terminus of the La'al Ratty railway
Grid ref: NY 173 007
Ordnance Survey Map: OL6 The English Lakes South-western area. Coniston, Ulverston & Barrow-in-Furness
After the walk: The Boot Inn and the Brook House Inn in Boot; Fellbites Café at Dalegarth Station

Walk outline

After a short section of road walking, the route leaves Boot and heads on to the open moorland. Compass and map-reading skills will be put to the test here as the paths are sometimes vague and boggy. Eel Tarn is visited first, after which we cross Lambford Bridge to reach Burnmoor Tarn near the foot of Scafell. Finally, an old corpse road, now a clear track, leads back to Boot.

Eel Tarn and Burnmoor Tarn

Far from the Lakeland honeypots, Eel Tarn and Burnmoor Tarn are found on the moody moorland above Eskdale. This area sees relatively few visitors of the human variety but is home to a wide range of bog-loving plants and creatures, as well as grazing livestock.

Secluded Eel Tarn

Walkers visit Eel Tarn first, a relatively small and shallow pool where dragonflies and damselflies thrive. Burnmoor Tarn, on the other hand, is a much larger body of water —the third largest tarn in the Lake District, in fact—and is located at more than 250 metres above sea level.

Red darter dragonfly

The Walk

1. Leave the station and turn left along the road and left again at the **Brook House Inn**. Just before the humpback bridge at the end of the road in **Boot**, turn right – along a track beside **Whillan Beck**.

You'll see Eskdale Mill on the opposite bank, the Lake District's last working water-powered corn mill. Following a £1 million restoration, largely thanks to Lottery money, both of its traditional waterwheels are back in working order. The site also has a new hydroelectric plant powered by Whillan Beck.

2. About 500 metres beyond the village, take the short track on the right leading to a gate. Once through this, turn left to climb beside the wall. A clearer path from the right is joined as you continue uphill with the wall. The route heads along a walled section of path above the farm at **Gill Bank** before entering more open country.

3. Immediately after passing beneath a small crag, the path crosses a tiny beck – **Eel Tarn**'s outlet stream. To make a quick, there-and-back visit to the tarn, follow this upstream. It's only about 150 metres to the edge of the swampy ground surrounding this tranquil body of

water. Having returned to the main path, continue in the same direction as before. At an indistinct fork, keep left. Almost immediately, the path disappears on the damp ground. Keep straight ahead, and you'll quickly pick it up again, heading roughly north-east.

Cattle crossing Burnmoor Tarn's shallow outflow

You need to pay close attention to the path in this area; it has a tendency to disappear for short stretches. A combination of nifty footwork and good balance are required when tackling the boulders across several shallow becks and areas of peaty ground. The route keeps to fairly level ground – passing below most of the **rock outcrops** – until it crosses **Brockshaw Beck**.

4. Beyond the beck, there's a short rise through the bracken. The path then becomes less obvious again. There are two faint trails heading north-west, both leading to the same place. Soon after they reunite, you'll see a split boulder to the left of the path and an old sheepfold a few yards up to the right. The route continues across drier, more level ground now—continuing north-west for a little longer before swinging north below **Great How**. *The Mosedale fells soon appear: Pillar the most prominent, with the scree slopes of Kirk Fell to the right of it.* Eventually, you'll see **Lambford Bridge** spanning **Whillan Beck** down to the left. Swing down to this when the path splits.

A beautiful summer's evening at Eel Tarn

5. Having crossed, head straight up the slope and, after about 90 metres, you'll reach a reasonably clear, but damp path. Turn right along this. *Scafell, England's second highest mountain, has appeared up to the right now, its summit dome a mess of scree and rocks.* At a faint fork, bear left (north-west), avoiding some seriously boggy ground on the main path. The bypass trail is vague, but maintain your direction and, after less than 150 metres, you'll step up on to a clearer path. Turn right here, eventually dropping to **Burnmoor Tarn**. Continue as far as **Bulatt Bridge**, which crosses its outlet stream.

6. Starting the return journey, turn around and retrace your steps for 370 metres. Nearing the trail that originally brought you on to this path, you'll see a path to the right. Ignore this. You'll then reach a junction. The narrow trail up from Lambford Bridge goes left, while the clearer route ahead splits in two. Take the left-hand option of these two. Having gained a little height, you can see Eel Tarn – a sheet of blue surrounded by green – on a shoulder to the south-east. About 1.6 kilometres beyond Bulatt Bridge, join a stonier path coming down from the right. Beyond a gate, the path continues beside a wall.

7. Having passed through several more gates, you reach a T-junction with a well-used path. Continue downhill on this. Dropping to a waymarked junction, go through the gate on the left. Walk past the restored mill seen earlier and over a bridge. Retracing your steps, walk through **Boot** to reach the road junction. Turn right, and the car park is on the right in 270 metres. ♦

Peat

Look up onto the fells as you descend into Boot at the end of the walk and you will see some 18th-century stone peat huts. Eskdale once relied heavily on peat for fuel. After cutting and leaving the peat to dry on the moor for several weeks, local families would transport it to the huts by horse-drawn sledge where it would be stored until it was needed in the winter.

Blea Tarn and the Langdale Pikes at first light

Blea Tarn

A short, but steep walk onto a low, rocky fell towered over by iconic Langdale peaks

What to expect:

Fell paths, including a narrow rock squeeze; tarn-side track

Distance/time: 4.5 kilometres/ 3 miles. Allow 2-2½ hours

Start: National Trust's Blea Tarn Pay and Display car park

Grid ref: NY 295 043

Ordnance Survey Map: OL 6 *The English Lakes South-western area. Coniston, Ulverston & Barrow-in-Furness*

After the walk: Old Dungeon Ghyll Hotel in Great Langdale

Walk outline

A steep, but mostly grassy path climbs to the 467-metre top of Lingmoor Fell. With fantastic views ahead, the route then follows the superb ridge. A rocky path hugs Side Pike's main buttress and passes through a narrow squeeze. After a short detour to the 344 metre summit, a faint path drops to the road. A constructed track then skirts Blea Tarn.

Blea Tarn

Photographers adore Blea Tarn. Poised with camera and tripod at the water's edge, they wait for the ideal moment to capture an image of this beautiful tarn with its immaculate backdrop. The bowl in which the tarn sits is gorgeous in itself—lightly wooded and with steep slopes to the east and west—but it is the Langdale Pikes, perfectly framed in the gap created by Blea Tarn Pass, that make this scene so idyllic.

This short but immensely satisfying walk heads onto the high ground to the east of the tarn, providing excellent views of the water below and the mountains ahead.

Bleatarn House

Fox

The Walk

1. Turn right out of the car park. Walk along the road for almost 300 metres and then take a faint path climbing the slope on your right. This heads towards a steep-sided gill, just before which it joins a clearer path coming up from the left. (If you should miss the initial turning off the road, continue a little further and then, just before you reach the whitewashed cottage of **Bleatarn House**, you will see a wall to the right of the road. Take the path climbing alongside this.) Whichever way you come off the road, follow the beck upstream, passing through a gap in a wall on the climb.

As you ascend, take some time to pause and enjoy the stunning mountain scenery: Wetherlam and Swirl How are over to the right; behind you, Crinkle Crags, Bowfell and the Langdale Pikes are clearly visible; and, all the while, Blea Tarn is down to the right.

2. Cross the stile in the next wall you encounter and continue uphill with the wall on your immediate left. The path is rough and stony, but it isn't long before you reach the ridge. Cross the stile in the fence and turn left to climb quickly to the cairn. This is **Brown How**, the highest point of Lingmoor Fell.

The outstanding views now also include the Helvellyn range, Fairfield, Windermere, the Pennines and Morecambe Bay.

3. Head downhill with the dilapidated wall/fence on your left and the mountains of **Langdale** straight ahead. Blea Tarn puts in an appearance far below from time to time as does Lingmoor Tarn, lying forgotten in the folds of the fell down to the right. There is a long

0   0.5km
¼ mile

5

Blind

6
224

Side Pike

Cattle Grid

4

Bleatarn
House
213

Rakerigg

Blea
Tarn

204

1 P
START

Birk
Knott

Brown
How

3

2

Mart
Crag

Tarnclose
Crag

Pits
(dis)

The Langdale Pikes towards the end of the walk

drop to Side Pike and the path is steep and rocky in places. It forks at a distinct left-hand kink in the fence. Take either route here: before too long, the right-hand path swings back round to the wall/fence, which continues to be your faithful companion, guiding you down some rough ground.

Drystone walls, such as the one snaking along this lovely ridge, are an integral part of Lakeland. The walls are built on a foundation of two parallel rows of large boulders on either side of a trench. The sides are then built up and the inside *is filled with smaller stones. At regular intervals, a layer of 'through stones' is placed across the width of the wall to strengthen it. Walls are generally topped with a row of slanting stones, known as 'cam-stones', to discourage sheep from climbing them.*

4. With the worst of the descent behind you, cross a stile in the wall on your left and continue downhill with the wall now on your right. This path takes you all the way to the base of **Side Pike's** formidable buttresses, straight ahead. Go through a kissing-gate in a fence

The Langdale Pikes form the perfect backdrop to Blea Tarn

and then continue up towards the steep rock face. Only as you reach the base of the crag does the path finally swing left to find a route around the southern side of the fell. It clings tightly to a ledge and squeezes its way through a narrow gap between the rocks. The path then swings right and climbs.

5. Just after the Langdales reappear, the path splits. Bear right for the short, easy climb to the summit of **Side Pike**, but the main route heads left. Follow the wall on your right until the path goes through a gap in it. With the ground ahead suddenly dropping away steeply,

the route is unclear. Basically, you need to pick up a path, cairned in places, that negotiates several shallow rocky ledges to descend in a mostly west-south-west direction. Nearing the base of the fell, this goes through one kissing-gate and then another, providing access to the road at **Blea Tarn Pass**.

6. Cross straight over and then, a few metres back from the road, go through the gate on the left to access a constructed path.

This is one of the Lake District National Park's 'Miles Without Stiles' route—paths specially constructed for people with

mobility problems. Sections of this one are suitable for people operating their own wheelchairs.

Before long, you have **Blea Tarn** on your left. At a T-junction, turn left to cross the footbridge over the outlet stream. This path comes out at the road opposite the car park to complete the walk. ♦

Old Dungeon Ghyll

The Old Dungeon Ghyll Hotel, owned by the National Trust since 1929, was known as Middlefell Inn at the end of the 19th century. Back then, horse-drawn coaches would bring visitors from Little Langdale over Blea Tarn Pass. They would stop at the top and blow their horn, a signal to get lunch or tea ready—the number of blasts informed the staff of the number of passengers requiring a meal.

Easedale Tarn and Blea Crag

Easedale & Codale Tarns

Two tarns—one popular with visitors, one hidden away; and a visit to lonely Tarn Crag

What to expect:
Clear paths as far as Codale Tarn, then open fell; one rocky section

Distance/time: 11 kilometres/ 7 miles. Allow 3-4 hours

Start: The beginning of the Easedale Road in Grasmere village—opposite the Sam Read bookshop

Grid ref: NY 337 076

Ordnance Survey Map: OL 6 *The English Lakes South-western area. Coniston, Ulverston & Barrow-in-Furness;* and OL 7 *The English Lakes South-eastern area. Windermere, Kendal & Silverdale*

After the walk: Various pubs and cafés in Grasmere

Walk outline

A well trodden path climbs beside the dramatic waterfalls of Sourmilk Gill to beautiful Easedale Tarn. Continuing further into the valley, the next target is Codale Tarn. A final grassy climb leads onto Tarn Crag, the highest and loneliest part of the walk. Paths are, at best, vague here. The route drops down a bracken-covered ridge and into Far Easedale where a good track leads back to Grasmere.

Easedale Tarn and Codale Tarn

Easedale Tarn has long been admired by visitors: in Victorian times, there was even a refreshments hut at the water's edge, serving light lunches and hot drinks. Its popularity is hardly surprising: it is situated in a lovely location 200 metres above Grasmere with steep slopes to the north and south-west.

Sourmilk Gill waterfalls

Codale Tarn, tucked into a quiet hollow in the fells below Codale Head, is another story. Equally attractive, but another 180 metres higher up the valley, there's a bit more effort required to reach it. Fewer people venture this far.

Common frog

The Walk

1. From the centre of **Grasmere**, walk along Easedale Road for nearly 700 metres until you see a small footbridge in the trees to your left. Cross this bridge—signposted 'Easedale Tarn'—and then a second, smaller bridge. Keep to the clear, beckside track until it goes through a gate.

2. Beyond this, cross the farm track diagonally right. After one final gate, the more sustained climbing begins. The path is a little rough and rocky in places, but the tumultuous waterfalls of **Sourmilk Gill** – a fearsome sight after heavy rain – provide a welcome distraction from any difficulties underfoot.

3. On reaching **Easedale Tarn**, follow the main path as it skirts the southern

side of the tarn and then begins to climb. The path is steep in places and you may need to use your hands for balance as you clamber up the bare rock just below **Belles Knott**. The gradient eventually eases as you reach a more open area.

4. Leave the main path here by turning right along a narrow trail that quickly drops to cross the beck and continues to **Codale Tarn**. The path skirts the water's edge before crossing the outlet stream and then continuing to the northern end of the tarn.

5. There are few obvious routes on the ground from now on, but there are some faint paths and, as long as you know how to use a map and compass, you shouldn't go wrong. Just before

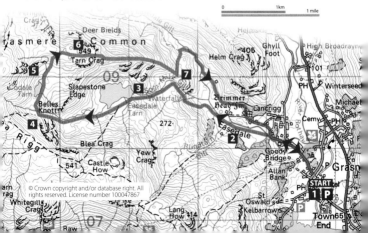

Looking down to Easedale Tarn from Belles Knott

reaching the inlet stream, bear right (north-east) away from the tarn. There is a faint path on the ground that runs parallel with the inlet stream—about 80 metres to the right of it, avoiding the boggy ground closer to the beck.

As you draw level with a sheepfold off to your left, you climb more steeply, now heading north up the grassy slope. On reaching the base of some craggier ground at the top of this rise, bear right (north-east) along a faint path skirting the rocky area to your left. Do not be tempted by the clearer path that swings left towards Codale Head. You quickly reach a faint crossing of paths where you turn right.

6. Just before the path starts dropping away more steeply, you will see a faint path off to the left. Take this for a quick detour onto the 485 metre summit of **Tarn Crag**.

Fairfield and the Helvellyn range dominate the scene to the north-east, but all eyes will inevitably be drawn to the charming view down Easedale and on to Grasmere.

To continue on the route, drop back to

Easedale Tarn rests in a lovely location 200 metres above Grasmere

the main path and then head steeply down a shallow, mostly grassy gully. Walkers' boots have created a faint zig-zagging path that will ease your descent.

At the bottom of this first drop, continue east along the faint, grassy ridge path. Don't be tempted by clearer paths heading off down to the right—although the worst that could happen would be that you'd end up back at Easedale Tarn. There are no right and wrong ways of descending this lonely ridge. There are faint paths all over the place—some stick to the highest

ground; some avoid the craggiest bits. It's a case of pick and mix. Choose the options that suit you best—and enjoy! In its lower stages, the ridge path descends through bracken.

7. On reaching a T-junction with a clearer path, turn left. You are unlikely to go wrong here—the route is obvious, there are yellow waymarkers to guide you and, just in case you are in any doubt, there is a huge boulder with 'Grasmere' and a large arrow painted on it.

8. Approaching the valley bottom in **Far Easedale**, veer right where a path

joins from the left. Cross the wooden footbridge and head downstream. You eventually lose the beck, but the way ahead is obvious. At a junction of tracks, keep straight ahead—signposted for 'Grasmere'. Go through the gate and walk down the lane. Swing left along the asphalt and follow the road back into **Grasmere village** to complete the walk. ♦

'The Black Quarter'

It's hard to escape from references to the Wordsworths in and around Grasmere—and Easedale Tarn is no exception. William and his sister Dorothy were frequent visitors to the tarn. They referred to the valley as 'the Black Quarter', claiming it was the source of all the bad weather that hit Grasmere. The Wordsworths lived in Grasmere for many years.

Styhead Tarn and Great End

Styhead & Sprinkling Tarns

A moderate walk beneath some of Lakeland's highest and most impressive mountains

What to expect:

Well-walked tracks and paths throughout, loose on the initial descent

Distance/time: 9 kilometres/ 5½ miles. Allow 3-4 hours

Start: Seathwaite in Borrowdale. The roadside parking leading to Seathwaite fills up early. Walkers may need to park in the National Trust Pay and Display car park in Seatoller, 2 kilometres away

Grid ref: NY235 123

Ordnance Survey Map: OL 4 *The English Lakes North-western area. Keswick, Cockermouth & Wigton;* and OL 6 *The English Lakes South-western area. Coniston, Ulverston & Barrow-in-Furness*

After the walk: Yew Tree Country Restaurant in Seatoller

Walk outline

Easy walking on a stony track beside Grains Gill leads to the Styhead Gill path. After a moderate ascent beside Taylorgill Force and then alongside the beck, the first of the tarns—Styhead Tarn—is reached. More climbing on a well-used track beneath Great End's mighty buttresses leads to Sprinkling Tarn. The long descent is via Ruddy Gill and Grains Gill. The path is badly eroded in places.

Styhead Tarn and Sprinkling Tarn

It's hard to match these two tarns for the drama and grandeur of their settings. Styhead Tarn sits at the base of the iconic Great Gable, with the fearsome eastern face of Lingmell dominating the scene. Get here early or late in the day, and there's a good chance there will be tents pitched beside the water, wild-campers enjoying some of the most beautiful mountain scenery in England.

Higher still, Sprinkling Tarn is renowned for being the wettest place in the country. Great End's mighty buttresses loom over this majestic body of water.

Stockley Bridge

Foxglove

The Styhead Gill path is used by walkers aiming for Scafell Pike

The Walk

1. Having parked on the Seathwaite road, walk south and follow the track into the farmyard and out the other end.

As you make your way up the valley on a clear, broad track, the slopes on your right belong to Base Brown, while those on the left lead up to Glaramara. The valley floor here is strewn with boulders, testament to the force of the beck when in flood. After heavy rainfall—and this area is prone to particularly high rain—it comes raging down from the mountains, spreading out across the valley floor and depositing its load of rocks. In dry weather, it's sometimes hard to make out exactly where the beck is among all this debris.

2. After crossing the humpback **Stockley Bridge**, go through a gate in a wall. Ignore the path to the left here (this forms part of the return route); instead, head straight up the well-trodden path. The gradient eases slightly as you pass beyond the tree-lined ravine that hides **Taylorgill Force**. Continue uphill beside **Styhead Gill**, crossing a footbridge just before you reach **Styhead Tarn**.

The clear path passes around the western side of the water.

Lingmell dominates the scene straight ahead, the dark gash of Piers Gill slicing beneath its inhospitable eastern face.

3. Before long you reach the Mountain Rescue stretcher box at Sty Head. Turn left here.

Some of the Lake District's busiest paths converge at this pass. Sit here and watch the world go by: climbers making their way to Napes Needle, hikers intent on Great Gable's south-eastern breast, charity walkers struggling up England's highest mountain. It's like...well...Piccadilly Circus!

At a faint fork in a short while, keep left—the path to the right is the popular Corridor Route to Scafell Pike. The loose, stony path climbs at a moderate angle to reach the edge of **Sprinkling Tarn**.

Most walkers will stride on past Sprinkling Tarn, hardly giving it a second glance as they continue up to Esk Hause, but it's worth pausing for a while here. The tarn is cradled between the many lumps and bumps of Seathwaite Fell. The area is dotted with tiny pools sparkling in hollows or hidden from view by encircling crags; and

with superb views of the surrounding mountains, it's an excellent spot to explore at a leisurely pace. Those with the time and the energy can take a stroll out to Seathwaite Fell's northern summit with superb

0 _____ 1km

1 mile

Styhead Tarn remains in shadow as dawn reaches the surrounding fells

views down to Seathwaite and across to Skiddaw in the distance.

Continue along the clear Esk Hause path beyond the tarn, below the huge gullies that dissect Great End's magnificent northern buttresses.

4. About 350 metres beyond the tarn, as the rock beneath your feet turns red, turn left to cross the gill. Follow **Ruddy Gill** and then **Grains Gill** downstream on a clear path, with the slopes of Seathwaite Fell up to your left at first. The badly eroded path can be rather loose underfoot in places, but various attempts have been made to repair it

over the years. The many interesting gullies, waterfalls and pools in the gills help relieve the tedium of the relentless downhill slog.

5. You eventually cross Grains Gill on a narrow wooden bridge. Turn right at the next path junction, going through a gate to recross **Stockley Bridge**. Now retrace your steps to **Seathwaite** to complete the walk.

On the way back into Seathwaite, you will see spoil heaps up on the slopes to the west. These belong to the now disused 'wad' mines. Wad is the local name for plumbago, more commonly known as

graphite. The discovery of graphite, early in the 16th century, gave rise, several hundred years later, to Keswick's famous pencil industry. According to local legend, it all started with a violent storm in Borrowdale, which led to trees being uprooted and the discovery of an unknown black material underneath. Shepherds then began using the mysterious substance to mark their sheep, creating the world's first pencils. ♦

Wet, wet, wet!

Seathwaite is famous for being the wettest inhabited place in the country. The rain gauge that measures rainfall here is located near Sprinkling Tarn. The biggest downpour ever recorded during one 24-hour period in the UK was at Sprinkling Tarn in November 2009—a massive 314 millimetres, or more than one foot of rain. The deluge resulted in catastrophic flooding on the River Derwent in Keswick, Cockermouth and Workington.

Looking across Innominate Tarn to Great Gable

Innominate Tarn

A stiff climb onto a popular fell surrounded by magnificent mountain scenery

What to expect:
Lakeshore paths, stony bridleway, rocky clamber, fell path

Distance/time: 12.5 kilometres/ 7½ miles. Allow 3½-4½ hours

Start: National Park Pay and Display car park behind the Bridge Hotel in Buttermere

Grid ref: NY 174 169

Ordnance Survey Map: OL 4 *The English Lakes North-western area. Keswick, Cockermouth & Wigton*

After the walk: Croft House Café, Bridge Hotel and Buttermere Court Hotel, all in Buttermere

Walk outline

The easy walk beside Buttermere makes for a gentle warm-up for the climb onto Haystacks. After ascending to Scarth Gap, the route clambers up the fell's rocky western ridge. On the summit, a well-used path keeps to the northern edge of the fell, passing Innominate Tarn along the way. The descent uses a relatively quiet path on the southern side of Warnscale Beck and then returns via the lake.

Innominate Tarn

This pretty, reedy tarn is one of many bodies of water hidden among the maze of crags and heathery knolls that make up Haystacks. Viewed from the west, it reflects the iconic Great Gable; and, from the east, craggy Pillar. A favourite with guidebook writer Alfred Wainwright, it was here that his ashes were scattered after his death in 1991.

Although the route description keeps close to the northern edge of Haystacks, it is worth taking your time and going off-track occasionally to explore this complex but wonderful landscape.

Haystacks' summit tarn

Wheatear

The Walk

1. Heading away from the main car park, turn right to follow the public bridleway to the left of the **Buttermere Court Hotel**—towards the lake. Passing through several gates and ignoring a path to Scale Bridge on the right,

2. As you draw level with the south-east end of the lake, leave the main path by bearing right to head towards a small conifer plantation. You are soon on the bridleway to Scarth Gap, linking the Buttermere valley with Ennerdale on the other side. As you ascend, don't be tempted to stay on the right-hand side of the wall that comes snaking steeply up from the valley below; you need to go through a gap soon after first encountering it. The path gets steeper and rougher underfoot as you toil uphill, until you finally reach **Scarth Gap**.

keep to this wide track as it winds its way to the lakeshore. After going through a gate providing access to the lake, turn right, soon crossing the outlet stream via a bridge. Cross a second bridge, go through the gate and then follow the lakeshore path. Whenever the route forks, keep left to enjoy spectacular views across **Buttermere**.

The view back to Buttermere from the path below Blackbeck Tarn

3. Turn left at a large cairn to the left of the path in the pass. This marks the start of the climb onto Haystacks—a stony staircase that winds its way up the fellside. It becomes increasingly steep and rocky, and you may need to use your hands on the more difficult sections.

4. The first tarn you come to after the main climb is truly 'innominate', in that it is not marked and therefore remains unnamed on most maps. The actual **Innominate Tarn** lies a further 600 metres to the south-east—in a depression between rocky, heathery knolls. To reach it, keep to the path along the northern edge of the fell.

After passing to the left of Innominate Tarn, the path swings left to descend slightly. It then cuts beneath a dark crag before crossing **Blackbeck Tarn**'s outlet stream.

Looking down the gully on the left here, there is a spectacular view to the green valley below, including Buttermere and Crummock Water.

Beyond the outlet stream, the path

High Crag from the unnamed tarn on the top of Haystacks

climbs again and then passes round the side of **Green Crag**. It is soon joined by another path and then crosses some damp ground. Before long, you will see a less well-used path to the right, heading off at a right angle to the main track. Our route swings left here, aiming, it seems, directly for the quarry workings on Fleetwith in the distance.

5. When the track then swings right again, leave it by turning left along a narrow path to begin the descent. This winds its way steadily to **Warnscale Bottom**, passing **Warnscale Bothy** along the way and cutting beneath

Haystacks' dark, northern cliffs. Cross the sturdy bridge over **Warnscale Beck** and follow the faint path up to a clear bridleway, along which you bear left.

6. Turn left at the road, soon passing **Gatesgarth Farm**, one of the largest privately-owned farms in the National Park. When you reach the lakeshore again, take the gravel path off to the left. This makes its way along the lakeshore, back towards the village, passing through a short, dark tunnel cut into the rock along the way.

7. At the western end of the lake, bear

right when the path splits. It goes through several gates and swings right —over rock. At the top of a fenced section, turn sharp left. The clear path passes between **farm buildings** to reach the road below **St James's Church**. Turn left and left again at the **Bridge Hotel**. Continue to the car park to complete the walk. ♦

The 'Beauty of Buttermere'

The Buttermere Court Hotel, formerly The Fish, was once home to Mary Robinson, the 'Beauty of Buttermere'. Praised in an early guide book, she was subsequently seduced by and married Colonel Alexander Hope, MP for Linlithgow. Sadly, soon after the wedding it was discovered that the real Colonel Hope was overseas. Mary had married an imposter—John Hatfield, wanted for forgery and bigamy. He was later arrested and hanged for his crimes.

Angle Tarn bathed in dawn light

Angle Tarn

A moderate walk to a tranquil tarn with great views of the Helvellyn range

What to expect:

Rough tracks and fell paths, which may be wet in places

Distance/time: 9.5 kilometres/ 6 miles. Allow 3-4 hours

Start: A small free parking area at the eastern end of Hartsop. There is alternative parking about a kilometre away, at Cow Bridge on the A592, near Brothers Water

Grid ref: NY 410 131

Ordnance Survey Map: OL 5 *The English Lakes North-eastern area. Penrith, Patterdale & Caldbeck*

After the walk: The Brotherswater Inn, 1.5km south of Hartsop

Walk outline

The initial climb beside the waterfalls of Hayeswater Gill is fairly gentle. From Hayeswater itself, though, it steepens and crosses damp ground to reach a high point of 556 metres near Satura Crag. With fantastic views west, a good path drops to Angle Tarn and then Boredale Hause. A rough track leads back into the valley where the walk ends with a quiet trail through ancient woods.

Angle Tarn

There are two Angle Tarns in the Lake District: one at the foot of Esk Pike and this one in the eastern fells, close to Ullswater. It is exquisitely located at 479 metres above sea level, tucked in at the base of Angletarn Pikes. On the route of Wainwright's Coast to Coast Walk, it's a popular spot with wild campers who wake to the glorious scene of Fairfield, St Sunday Crag and the Helvellyn range lit up by the morning sun.

As well as superb views, the walk provides plenty of interest, including a visit to one of the Lake District's prettiest hamlets.

Track to Hayeswater

Sundew

The Walk

1. Go through the gate at the far end of the car park and walk along the clear track—signposted to 'Hayeswater'. After crossing a cattle grid, the track forks. Bear right and descend to **Hayeswater Gill**, crossing via a bridge.

It's hard to imagine it now, but this used to be a busy lead mining area. The scant remains of Low Hartsop mine are visible nearby, at the confluence of Hayeswater Gill and Pasture Beck. Stone piers and a wheel pit are all that remain of a huge water wheel constructed to drain the mine, which suffered badly from flooding. The works were abandoned in 1878.

2. The wide, stony track climbs beside **Hayeswater Gill**, and its tumbling waterfalls.

3. As the gill opens out, cross the bridge on the left. A constructed path swings right, quickly going over to grass. *You'll soon see **Hayeswater** ahead, beautifully located in a bowl between Gray Crag and the Straits of Riggindale. This body of water was, until recently, a reservoir. United Utilities removed the old weir dam in 2014, restoring the tarn's natural flow.* Having swung back round to the

The sun's first rays illuminate Angle Tarn

left, the path aims for an old wall. Damp in places, it then makes a more direct assault on the grassy hillside, following the line of the wall on the left.

4. On reaching a constructed path, turn left, quickly crossing what remains of the wall.

You are now on the route of Alfred Wainwright's Coast to Coast Walk from St Bees on Cumbria's coast to Robin Hood's Bay on the North Yorkshire coast. The famous guidebook writer devised this 190-mile route in 1973. Crossing some of England's most beautiful scenery, including

three National Parks, it is now one of the most popular long-distance walks in the world.

As you wind your way through an area of rocky outcrops near **Satura Crag**, keep close to the drystone wall/fence that recently came in from the left.

The views to the west, which have been gradually improving since you left the reservoir, are now absolutely superb. The amazing panorama of mountains includes Hart Crag, the dark, eastern cliffs of Fairfield, St Sunday Crag and the Helvellyn range. Take some time to enjoy

Superb views to Deepdale, Fairfield and the Helvellyn range

the views to the east too—the long line of misty hills that can be seen in the distance from time to time is the Pennines.

5. Just after going through a gap in a drystone wall, you will see **Angle Tarn** below. Ignoring any trails to the right, keep to the clear path as it descends to the water and then swings left to ascend slightly. Keep left at a faint fork and the ground on your left will soon drop away, revealing jaw-dropping views down the steep slopes into the upper reaches of Patterdale and across to lonely Deepdale. This superb path hugs the edge of the fell and then drops into a shallow gap between the hills.

6. Having crossed a small beck on stepping stones, you reach a flat, grassy area at **Boredale Hause**. Continue in roughly the same direction to pick up a descending track that immediately splits in two. Bear left here. This track is steep and loose in its early stages, but things improve as you descend.

7. Bear left at a track junction close to the valley bottom. Just before you reach the bridge over **Angletarn Beck**, bear left up a faint path heading towards the beck. Ford it just a few metres upstream of the bridge. On the other side of the small gate, keep to the clearest path at all times. After an area of woodland, the

path all but disappears in the mud, but persevere: head up the tiny outcrop of rock and you will pick it up again as it passes beneath a small crag and then through a gate. Turn left along the vehicle track, which climbs briefly before dropping down into **Hartsop**. Turn left along the lane and walk through the hamlet. Return to the car park to complete the walk. ◆

Red deer

These fells are home to England's oldest native herd of red deer, said to be the only herd that hasn't cross-bred with sika deer. The ancient deer forest itself is centred on The Nab.

In autumn, listen for the deep roaring of the stags in rut. These enormous males, who congregate in single-sex herds for much of the year, have now gone their separate ways and are gathering their harems for the mating season.

Red Tarn and Swirral Edge

Red Tarn

Magnificent views of valleys and fells on this outstanding walk to a high mountain tarn

What to expect:
Rough tracks and fell paths, mostly good underfoot

Distance/time: 10.5 kilometres/ 6½ miles. Allow 3½-4½ hours

Start: Main National Park Pay and Display car park in Glenridding

Grid ref: NY 386 169

Ordnance Survey Map: OL 5 *The English Lakes North-eastern area. Penrith, Patterdale & Caldbeck*

After the walk: Choice of pubs and cafés in Glenridding

Walk outline

The climb to Red Tarn is long, but the climbing is well spaced-out, with only one or two steep sections. The paths as far as Lanty's Tarn are well walked, but the next section of the ascent is on a wonderful, little-used trail with superb views up Grisedale. Constructed paths lead from the ridge to Red Tarn and down to Glenridding Beck. A delightful leat route, hugging the side of the fell high above the valley floor, then takes you most of the way back to Glenridding.

Red Tarn

Red Tarn is spectacularly situated at the bottom of the cliffs of Helvellyn's east face, cradled between the mountain's two famous arêtes, Striding Edge and Swirral Edge. At 718 metres above sea level, it's the sixth highest tarn in the Lake District and home to brown trout and the rare schelly.

Taking in the impressive Grisedale and Glenridding valleys, the walk is pure delight from beginning to end—using excellent paths with fantastic views of the surrounding craggy mountains.

Grisedale

Raven

The Walk

1. From the car park, head back out onto the main road and turn right. Turn right again along a surfaced lane immediately after crossing the bridge over **Glenridding Beck**. Bear left at a fork in the track. At the next set of cottages, take the path on the left – signed to 'Lanty's Tarn and Helvellyn'.

The route crosses a small bridge, goes through a gate and then swings right to climb through the woods, soon joined by the alternative path coming up from the right. The next gate provides access to bracken-covered slopes and you now have a superb view across the valley to your right. The path forks just before another small gate. Bear left here, away from the gate.

2. You soon go through a larger wooden gate to access **Lanty's Tarn**, a calm stretch of water surrounded by trees. The path skirts the edge of the tarn. Immediately after the **dam**, take the narrow trail on the right. Keep to the right of two small rock outcrops and make your way to an area of woodland.

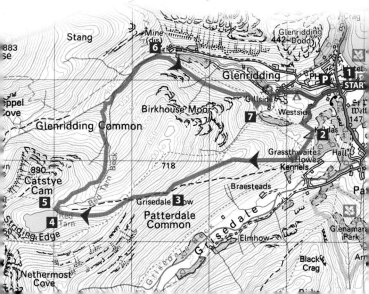

Looking down on Red Tarn from Striding Edge

Enter via a tall gate. About 40 metres after leaving the woods, there is a solitary pine on the left. Bear right here, soon ascending steeply. Another path joins from the right. Keep right at a faint fork, staying with the higher path with its superb perspective on glorious Grisedale.

The way ahead becomes less obvious after a gate and stile. Head west-south-west and it becomes slightly clearer again as it passes a rock outcrop on the right and winds its way up to a small saddle. You will see a wall to the right but resist any trails leading up to it.

Down to the left is the well-worn path that leads from Patterdale to Striding Edge. You will eventually drop down to this, but for now delight in the seclusion of this higher path and its views.

3. Reaching a fence, drop left and then continue your uphill journey on the main path. When you reach the ridge, climb the ladder stile in front of you. On the other side, take the path directly ahead, heading away from the wall—straight towards **Helvellyn.**

4. Red Tarn is hidden from view from the main path. To reach the water's

Red Tarn with Striding Edge on one side and Swirral Edge on the other

edge, bear left when the constructed track negotiates its way through a slightly rockier area.

Sitting at the foot of England's third highest mountain, this is a great place to rest and watch the walkers on Striding Edge up to the left. There have been many accidents, many of them fatal, along this narrow arête over the years.

The exit from the ridge, in fact, is marked by a plaque telling the story of artist Charles Gough, whose body was found in 1805 at the base of the crags beneath this spot. His rotting remains had been guarded for three months by his dog.

5. When you reach the outlet stream, cross and bear right. The path quickly broadens as it swings left and reaches a junction. Go right to begin the stony descent. About 1.8 kilometres from the tarn, cross **Red Tarn Beck** via a small, wooden bridge and then continue with **Glenridding Beck** on your left.

6. About 200 metres after passing and ignoring a bridge over the beck, you will see a faint, grassy path off to the left. Ignore this. Instead, stay on the clear, level path that follows the line of a disused leat. Do not leave this until you come to a wall apparently blocking your

way ahead. Bear left here to descend a rocky path. At the bottom of the short descent, turn right.

7. Go through a gate and follow the track down to a lane. Turn left and

then turn right along a wide track just before the bridge across the beck. This leads back into **Glenridding village** to complete the walk. ♦

Greenside Mine

Lead was discovered at Greenside in the 17th century, but serious development didn't begin until 1822. By 1849, there were 300 workers here, making it the largest lead mine in England. It was the first mine in Britain to use electrical winding, generating its own electricity with water turbines. The rushing water was supplied by the damming of tarns. The mine closed in 1962.

The path down to Bowscale Tarn

Bowscale Tarn

A steady ascent on to the moody moorland of the Northern Fells and a visit to a perfect corrie tarn

What to expect:
Road; tracks; grassy path on open fell; steep descent to tarn

Distance/time: 9.5 kilometres/ 6 miles. Allow 3-4 hours

Start: Bowscale Moss parking area just south of Mosedale, near Mungrisdale

Grid ref: NY 359 316

Ordnance Survey Map: OL 5 *The English Lakes North-eastern area. Penrith, Patterdale & Caldbeck*

After the walk: Mill Inn at Mungrisdale

Walk outline

After a short section on road, the route heads into the hills at Mungrisdale. It follows the River Glenderamackin upstream briefly before climbing a good path on to the open moorland. Walkers now head up and over the grassy dome of Bowscale Fell, which enjoys great views back to Skiddaw and Blencathra. After the route drops steeply to Bowscale Tarn, a track then leads back to the road.

Bowscale Tarn

Once popular with Victorian tourists, Bowscale Tarn is silent now, an oasis of solitude and serenity in a National Park that receives over 15 million visitors each year. Hardly ever seeing the sun in winter, it hides in a perfect glacial bowl at the foot of Bowscale Fell and is ringed on one side by moody cliffs.

This walk drops steeply on to this atmospheric spot from above, from the lofty moorland of the lonely Northern Fells, having first climbed the 702 metres (2,303ft) Bowscale Fell, a broad-backed hill typical of this part of the Lake District.

River Glenderamackin

Buzzard

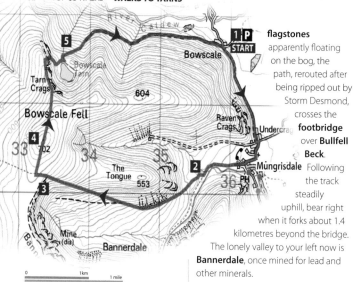

The Walk

1. From the parking area, walk south along the minor road into **Mungrisdale**. After entering the village, turn right along a rough track beside a 'phone box. The wide track goes through a large gate and heads towards the hills. *You'll see the River Glenderamackin over to the left. During the storms of December 2015, this raged through the valley, destroying much of the local path infrastructure.*

2. After negotiating some **massive flagstones** apparently floating on the bog, the path, rerouted after being ripped out by Storm Desmond, crosses the **footbridge** over **Bullfell Beck**. Following the track steadily uphill, bear right when it forks about 1.4 kilometres beyond the bridge. The lonely valley to your left now is **Bannerdale**, once mined for lead and other minerals.

3. As the ascent levels off, be careful not to be lured left by the lovely path that swings south-west along the edge of the high ground. Instead, head west-north-west along a narrow trail through the long grass. Then, in another 200 metres, bear right at a fork.

It doesn't matter if you miss this fork; either way, in less than 40 metres, you'll reach a wider path along which you turn right (north-north-east). You're now making directly for **Bowscale Fell**. The first thing you encounter on the top of the fell is the **summit shelter**. From here, continue to the **summit cairn**.

Bowscale Tarn is cradled by fells

4. From the summit cairn, there are two paths heading down the other side of the fell. Take the less distinct one to the left. As the path swings north-north-west, it approaches the edge of steep ground dropping down to Bowscale Tarn to the right. The route eventually descends this steep ground, but not until **Tarn Crags** has been bypassed. Only as the path ahead becomes even less distinct should you turn right and begin your descent on a clear path.

5. Having dropped to **Bowscale Tarn,** cross the outlet stream and turn left on the clear path. This leads back to the minor road where the walk started. At the end of the track, bear right to return to the parking area to complete the walk. ◆

Fell ponies

Fell ponies wander the road between Bowscale and Mungrisdale.
These friendly creatures trace their history back to the Romans, when indigenous ponies bred with those introduced by the occupiers. In the 13th century, with the rise of the wool trade, they began to be used as pack animals. Come the Industrial Revolution, they carried lead and iron ore from the fells to the smelting works on the north-east coast.

Useful Information

Cumbria Tourism

Cumbria Tourism's official website covers everything from accommodation and events to attractions and adventure. www.golakes.co.uk

Lake District National Park

The Lake District National Park website also has information on things to see and do, plus maps, webcams and news. www.lakedistrict.gov.uk

Tourist Information Centres

The main TICs provide free information on everything from accommodation and travel to what's on and walking advice.

Ambleside	015394 32582	amblesidetic@southlakeland.gov.uk
Grasmere	015394 35245	grasmeretic@lake-district.gov.uk
Bowness	015394 42895	bownesstic@lake-district.gov.uk
Coniston	015394 41533	mail@conistontic.org
Keswick	017687 72645	keswicktic@lake-district.gov.uk
Penrith	01768 867 466	pen_tic@eden.gov.uk
Ullswater	017684 82414	ullswatertic@lake-district.gov.uk
Windermere	015394 46499	info@windermereinfo.co.uk

Steamers and Ferries

Four lakes have regular, year round, steamers, launches or ferries.

Windermere	015395 43360	www.windermere-lakecruises.co.uk
		info@windermere-lakecruises.co.uk
Derwentwater	017687 72263	www.keswick-launch.co.uk
		info@keswick-launch.co.uk
Coniston	015394 32733	www.nationaltrust.org.uk/steam-yacht-gondola
		sygondola@nationaltrust.org.uk
	017687 75753	www.conistonlaunch.co.uk
		info@conferry.co.uk
Ullswater	017684 82229	www.ullswater-steamers.co.uk
		enquiries@ullswater-steamers.co.uk

Weather

Five day forecast for the Lake District: 0844 846 2444

www.lakedistrict.gov.uk/weatherline

LIFE'S LITTLE DESTRUCTION BOOK

By Wayne Kerr

Illustrations by Mariusz at Caricatoons

220 Nicholson Road, Subiaco WA 6008, Australia
Tel: (09) 388 2062   Fax: (09) 388 2069

Angus&Robertson
An imprint of HarperCollins*Publishers*

An Angus & Robertson Publication

Angus&Robertson, an imprint of
HarperCollins*Publishers*
25 Ryde Road, Pymble, Sydney, NSW 2073, Australia
31 View Road, Glenfield, Auckland 10, New Zealand
77-85 Fulham Place Road, London W6 8JB, United Kingdom

First published in Australia in 1992 by Wayne Kerr
This edition 1993

ISBN 0 207 18337 6

Printed in Australia by The Australian Print Group

9 8 7 6 5 4 3 2 1
97 96 95 94 93

INTRODUCTION

THIS BOOK began after my third marriage break-up. None of them would toe the line, so they had to go!

As a former giver, and now a receiver, I realised the only way to survive in this cesspool we call life was to have a plan, a road map, a guide to lead us through the vicious nineties – already strewn with the bodies of nice guys who finished last.

This book lists 166 "must dos" to keep you severely out of step with ordinary people. It will show you how to become a stand-out person, ready to take advantage of every situation, and to cleanse yourself of sentimentality, good manners, thoughtfulness, politeness, and all that other limiting behaviour that has kept you in check all these years.

Cut a clean swathe through the little people.

After a bout with this volume you'll be able to cut a clean swathe through the "little people", with their conventional morality and accepted standards, and succeed beyond your most avaricious dreams by making material gains at the expense of others.

It's greed you need! Go ahead and be supreme in your isolation. You deserve it.

Wayne Kerr

1 ♦ Avoid self-help books like *"Life's Little Instruction Book."*

2 ♦ See if you can get this book without paying for it.

3 ♦ Be the first to say, "That's mine".

4 ♦ Enjoy interrupting the punchlines of other people's jokes.

5 ♦ Beware the outstretched hand.

6 ♦ Exploit at least three people a day. It will make yours.

7 ◆ Own a pit bull terrier. Keep it hungry.

8 ◆ Chase ambulances at every opportunity, especially if you're stuck in a traffic jam.

9 ◆ Foreplay is for wimps. And just remember that old definition of eternity: "The period between the time you cum and the time she leaves."

10 ◆ Develop a vise-like handshake.

11 ◆ Avoid eye contact.

12 ◆ Never be grateful. It's a sign of weakness.

13 ◆ Learn to cheat well at cards and golf.

14 ◆ Learn to trick your dog.
It's a great stress reliever at the end
of a hard day.

15 ◆ Don't be ashamed to live beneath
your dignity.

16 ◆ Drive an expensive car, and sleep around
to pay for it.

17 ◆ Never return library books.

18 ◆ Never forgive, never forget.

19 • Always attack from behind.

20 • Always borrow, never lend.

21 • Make new enemies but *don't forget* the old ones.

22 • Watch your back.

23 • Learn to tell lies based on elements of the truth.

24 • Be indiscreet.

25 • Broadcast your conquests.

26 ◆ Enjoy tormenting animals and children. Another top stress reliever.

27 ◆ Never write "thank-you" notes.

28 ◆ Never give anyone anything.

29 ◆ Never give up on anybody. Revenge is sweet.

30 ◆ Show respect only for men with guns.

31 ◆ Let others wash up. It's a waste of your time.

32 ◆ Never be afraid to show your rage.

Frame someone you really, really despise.

33 • Steal fruit from the back of trucks with hand-lettered signs.

34 • Never vote. It will never make a difference to your life.

35 • Give gifts you know they'll give back.

36 • No matter what the circumstances, never accept blame. Never, never take responsibility.

37 • Frame someone you really, really despise.

38 · Spend 10 per cent more than you earn. Just let the bills mount up, as you won't have to pay most of them. (See No. 66).

39 · Make the worst of a good situation.

40 · Offer to pick up your neighbour's mail while they're away. Then arrange for an accomplice to burgle their house.

41 · Use your wit to abuse, not amuse.

42 · Remember that someone else's bad news can be good news for you.

43 ♦ Always jump the traffic queue.

44 ♦ Never volunteer for anything.

45 ♦ Be nasty. Even if you're not, pretend to be. People will respect you more.

46 ♦ Exploit a charity in your community and become dependent on it.

47 ♦ Take everyone for granted.

48 ♦ Accept any job that pays more than you're worth.

49 ♦ Don't mess with model aircraft, and don't associate with those that do.

50 ♦ Slow pay.

51 ♦ In business and in family relationships, remember that the most important thing is, "What's in it for me?".

52 ♦ Forget the Joneses. Keep up with the Iwasakis.

53 ♦ Get the best lawyer and accountant money can buy.

54 ◆ Never encourage anyone to become a patriot.

55 ◆ Even if you're financially well-to-do, *always* cry poor.

56 ◆ Avoid environmentally-friendly people.

57 ◆ Buy things by phone using someone else's credit cards.

58 ◆ Smile a lot. People will think you're a nice person.

Deprive someone of hope. It might be all they have.

59 ◆ Buy the cheapest wine when invited to dinner parties. Substitute the price tag with a higher price tag.

60 ◆ When someone is relating an important event that's happened to them, top them with a story of your own.

61 ◆ Always hog the limelight.

62 ◆ Change your locks regularly.

63 ◆ Deprive someone of hope. It might be all they have.

64 ◆ When negotiating your salary, think of what you want, then double it.

65 ◆ Give yourself an hour to cool off before responding to someone who crosses you. Use the time to plot revenge.

66 ◆ Never pay your bills if you can get away with it. Creditors often can't be bothered to go to the expense of collecting smaller amounts.

67 ◆ Never give people the benefit of the doubt.

68 • Keep people waiting. They'll think you are more important than you are.

69 • Never be afraid to rip-off other people's ideas.

70 • Encourage your children to take a part-time job after the age of six. It will save you money.

71 • Never give people a second chance.

72 • Never be romantic. It's a waste of time and money.

73 ♦ Park in spaces reserved for the handicapped. If caught, act like you are mentally retarded – nine times out of ten you'll pull it off.

74 ♦ Return borrowed vehicles with the petrol tank empty, but humbly apologise.

75 ♦ Loosen up. Relax. Nothing is important, even rare life-and-death matters.

76 ♦ Criticize in public. Show who's boss.

77 ♦ Praise in private. It avoids others getting big heads.

78 ◆ Enjoy discussing money with people who have far less than you.

79 ◆ Have no respect whatsoever for tradition.

80 ◆ Never wave at children on school buses.

81 ◆ Learn to look mean, even if you don't feel like it. You'll gain the respect of all you meet.

82 ◆ Always hire people you can control and manipulate.

83 ◆ Avoid people like yourself. They're a threat.

Don't believe that money can't buy you happiness. It can.

84 · Don't believe that money can't buy you happiness. It can.

85 · No matter how sticky the situation, keep your cool.

86 · Never underestimate your power to control other people.

87 · Never try to see things from other people's point of view. It's irrelevant.

88 · Don't be afraid to burn bridges. There are plenty more rivers to cross.

89 ◆ Keep your overheads low.

90 ◆ Accept pain and disappointment as part of *other* people's lives.

91 ◆ Take advantage of people when they ask you to be honest with them.

92 ◆ Learn to handle a lead pipe.

93 ◆ Contribute five per cent of your income to a charity *you* control and claim it as a tax deduction.

94 ◆ When having contracts drawn up, make sure the fine print is illegible.

95 ◆ Remember, a foot in the door is worth two on the street.

96 ◆ Don't say you don't have enough time. You have exactly the same number of hours per day that were given to Attila The Hun, Joe McCarthy, Al Capone and Joe Stalin.

97 ◆ Avoid health clubs.

98 ◆ Don't delay acting on a good scam. Chances are someone else has just thought of it too. Success comes to the one who gets in first.

99 ◆ Remember that losers do what winners *avoid* like the plague.

100 ◆ Keep the knives sharp.

101 ◆ Listen to other people's problems. They could be your opportunities.

102 ♦ Beware of investigative journalists. Make sure you have easy access to the back door.

103 ♦ Be uncontactable when someone needs your help.

104 ♦ Rain on other people's parades.

105 ♦ Every day look for some small way to undermine your boss.

106 ♦ Whenever possible acquire things the old-fashioned way: Borrow or steal.

Remember no one makes it alone. Use others.

107 • Remember no one makes it alone. Use others.

108 • Save money. Use other people's.

109 • Forget committees. Scams work better when you work alone.

110 • Understand that happiness is not based on relationships with people you love and respect, but on *money* and *power*.

111 • Never buy expensive shoes, ties and belts. Borrow them from others.

112 · Drive a black car. People will fear and respect you.

113 · Street musicians and charity collectors are a pest. Avoid them and save your pennies.

114 · Support the unemployed. They are an unlimited source of exploitation.

115 · Never buy a pet. It costs more to keep a pet than a child.

116 ♦ When lunching with four or more people, offer to collect the money then pay the *exact* bill. Chances are, you'll get your meal paid for out of *their* tips.

117 ♦ Avoid advertising agencies unless you want to spend 25% more than you would without one on ads that nobody understands anyway.

118 ♦ After experiencing *good* service, food or products, make a scene *anyway*. If you're lucky you may not be charged.

119 • Don't worry about your reputation.
There are plenty of people who've never
heard of you yet.

120 • Tailgate. Other cars will soon get out of
your way.

121 • Don't allow self-pity.
The moment this emotion strikes,
do something nasty to someone more
fortunate than you.

122 ◆ Claim the credit for any success, even if you had little to do with it. The more you say it, the more others will believe you. (Even the person whose idea it was).

123 ◆ Never keep a mistress or girlfriend for *more* than one year. She may start to think about claiming *half* your assets.

124 ◆ Never be seen with your mistress or girlfriend in public. So if she does make any claim, deny *ever* having met her.

Every person that you meet knows something you don't.
Pick their brains then move on.

125 ◆ Have a friend who owns a truck. You'll save heaps on removal charges.

126 ◆ Make a list of twenty things you want to experience in your life. Leave your wife and kids and go for it.

127 ◆ It's better to give than receive. Unless we're talking about money or possessions.

128 ◆ Every person that you meet knows something you don't. Pick their brains then move on.

129 • Never tip.

130 • Don't be afraid to compromise your integrity.

131 • When planning a family trip abroad, rent a travel video about the places you'll visit — then cancel the trip.

132 • It pays to know influential cops.

133 • Never play Scrabble.

134 • Life was never meant to be easy for others.

135 ◆ Ingratiate yourself to rich old sick people. (Where there's a will, there's a chance).

136 ◆ Work in teams.

137 ◆ Keep the answering machine on, even when you're at home.

138 ◆ Never take phone calls. Ring them back so *you* have the advantage.

139 ◆ Once you've sold, shut up.

140 ◆ Learn to say sincerely, "You won't regret this".

141 ◆ Never trust anyone who says, "Trust me".

142 ◆ Always eat at food halls. You'll save heaps.

143 ◆ Better still, if dining alone, dress down and visit your local soup kitchen.

144 ◆ Always have an unlisted home telephone number.

145 ◆ Have at least 12 different business cards that you can use for *any* occasion.

146 ♦ Get a mobile phone, fax and pager.
That way you cut overheads and you keep
total control of things. The good thing is
that you are safe from annoying creditors
and hawkers.

147 ♦ Live so that when your children think of
fairness, caring and integrity, they think
of Uncle Bill.

148 ♦ During a garbage strike, gift wrap your
rubbish and leave on the back seat of your
unlocked car. It will soon be stolen.

Save your long distance calls 'til you're in someone else's home.
(Parties are a good time).

149 ♦ At Telethons, pledge lots of money on behalf of a person or company in your firing line. Insist that it's announced on air.

150 ♦ Always disrupt your ex-wives' new relationships. After all, they made *your* life miserable.

151 ♦ Save your long distance calls 'til you're in someone else's home. (Parties are a good time).

152 ♦ Discreetly spread lies about your office rivals. (Hint at homosexuality).

153 ♦ Respect entrepreneurs who've ripped off the public.

154 ♦ If you damage someone's vehicle when the owner is absent, always pretend to leave a note if there are witnesses. That way they won't think to get your number plate.

155 ♦ In establishing your prowess say, "I only have four inches, but width isn't everything".

156 ◆ Always remember the motto "Find 'em, F★★★ 'em, forget 'em".

157 ◆ If your child comes third in a school race, chastise him with, "We don't play for Bronze".

158 ◆ Beware the tin that rattles: Charity begins at home.

159 ◆ Make the most of other people's physical deficiencies.

160 ◆ Be cruel to be kind.

161 • Never admit your mistakes.

162 • Live life to the full.

163 • Marry only for money.

164 • Remember, women love bastards.

165 • As Attila The Hun said on his deathbed when asked if he could live his life again, would he change anything: "Yes, next time no more Mr Nice Guy".

166 • There is no 166. I lied. (What would you expect?).

Got a great suggestion for Edition 2?

You too can be infamous if your suggestion is included in my next edition. (Successful entries will be credited).

My suggestion:

My Name... **State**...........

Naturally, you won't be paid, but losers never are.
Send to: Wayne Kerr, PO Box 699, West Perth, WA 6872, Australia